Slow Joy

Slow Joy

Stefanie Marlis

The University of Wisconsin Press

The University of Wisconsin Press
114 North Murray Street
Madison, Wisconsin 53715

3 Henrietta Street
London WC2E 8LU, England

5 4 3 2 1

Printed in the United States of America

Library of Congress Cataloging-in-Publication Data
Marlis, Stefanie, 1951–
Slow joy/Stefanie Marlis.
80 pp. cm.
I. Title.
PS3563.A6735S57 1989 89-40260
811'.54—dc20

For Eliot, Caroline, Steve, Jane & Mike,
for my friends

Contents

Acknowledgments ix

I

Rhodos: Traveling 3
Chinese Bowls 5
Shift 6
Corner 7
Ars Poetica 8
Temple 9
Possibilities 10
Banner Of Fish 11
Singing It Back 12

II

Revolution 15
Next Door 16
The West Wall 17
The World Is Not Moved 18
Designs 19
Turning From The News 20
Living On The Hallelujah Side 21
The Hundredth One 22
Impressionism 23
Weapons 24
Building 25

III

Remembering About Love 29
Light And Choice 30
Fruit 31
15½ 32
Twin Bells, Three Red Peaches 33
The Same Orbit 34

Pattern Language 35
California Lottery 36
Hammer Then An Angel 37
We Have This Harmony 38
Heavy Equipment 39
Walks Of Life: 40
Weight Lifter 40
Psychic Healer 41
Masseuse 42
Beautician 43
Garbage Collector 44
Zoo Keeper 45
Geologist 46
Patient 47
Gospel Singer 48

IV
Abbott's Lagoon 51
McClure's Beach 52
Enough 53
Grace 54
Orange Blossoms 55
The Force Of His Sadness 56
Squaw Valley Without You 57
Hunger 58
We Women 59
Inevitable Her Hunger 60
The Child 61
Pure And Indiscriminate 62
The Light All Inside Them 63
Two, Three 64
Bells 65
Sail 66
Precious Few 67
Trespass 68
Presence And Absence 69

Acknowledgments

American Poetry Review: "Building"
Barque: "Inevitable Her Hunger" and "Light And Choice"
Bellingham Review: "The Same Orbit" and "Squaw Valley Without You"
Big Moon: "Enough"
Black Warrior Review: "The Force of His Sadness," "The Light All Inside Them" ("The Same Light"), "Remembering About Love"
5 A.M.: "Impressionism"
Five Fingers Review: "Psychic Healer," "Temple," "Two Three"
Floating Island: "Abbott's Lagoon" and "Trespass"
Hayden's Ferry Review: "15½"
Ironwood: "The Child," "Corner," "Hammer Then an Angel," "Possibilities," "Precious Few," "Presence and Absence," "Rhodos Traveling," "Sail," "Singing It Back," "We Have This Harmony"
Massachusetts Review: "Banner of Fish" and "Fruit"
Minnesota Review: "Turning From the News"
Poetry East: "Revolution," "We Women," "The World Is Not Moved"
Raccoon: "The Hundredth One" and "Patient"
Seattle Review: "Pattern Language"
Slow Lorris Reader: "Twin Bells, Three Red Peaches" ("Sentiment")
Sonora Review: "Chinese Bowls" ("Starlight"), "Zoo Keeper," "Shift"
Tendril: "Weapons"
Three Penny Review: "Weight Lifter"
Zyzzyva: "Masseuse"

Some of these poems appeared in a chapbook, *Red Tools,* published by Dooryard Press.

I

Rhodos: Traveling

I mean when we eat & sleep: what if we liberated the journey,
so that the day was not a name but a string of beads
warmed by the friction of the hand.

In this frail light which gains strength as the sun goes down
the room is not generous and I roam through the past,
as if the familiar was what kept me from letting go.
Where is the flat world, the one with sea monsters & gold?
How do we manage to love each other this way? One instant here,
another at a beach?

The sun gliding through the ruins above us
we swim in our shorts & t-shirts in the Aegean.
The fluorescent palps of the octopus in a cloud of fish
stream like a banner. The old man at the hotel, proud,
holds up his catch, shiny with brine & blood. And we are proud,
touching each other constantly
and sleeping through the rain in the beach grass,
the lights of the boats as near as the stars.

In the royal museum we are startled
by how the pebbles in the atrium roar
under our steps. Above us, ferns hanging in ancient pots,
the light labored into the skin of the statues.
We sit down to eat figs and plan the next day and going home:
first by boat past the white island, then by plane.

To deliberate over our travels,
but in some way be blind to the world,
in the way a hand which must see comes to know
the shape of the body—the translated words: long, mouth, scar.
The light sailing unregarded.

And what if when we traveled out of our bodies
we abandoned, too, that hovering near the ceiling of the room?
That watching me.
Felt the planted, unplanted: the fern leaf without form:
a glass passing through the table; octopus, ship, city
traveling through our very large hands.

Chinese Bowls

Butter melting on the knife at breakfast,
a deer by the stone wall makes no sound. Eliot sleeping.
But things without harmony? In Virgil's *Georgics*
the wonder is in things unlike: the muscled oxen
and the delicate bells & fruit of the field.
For the ancients all unlikely things joined in the stars:
the goddesses charted among the bears & snakes.
And don't things come to harmony? As when you judge someone
by how she dresses or keeps house, and then
come to see you are alike.
I have been going around memories: climbing a flight of stairs
from the city street into the quiet disorder of your apartment:
your clothes, books, the Chinese bowl you drank from. Things
that come to likeness. So the bear the bull
the dog. Starlight. So a child at the zoo asks, if she came back
would she be a zebra, a tiger?

Shift

The tree through the window begins to dissolve. The light is shaking.
5 6 7, you count the fruit that appears & disappears before your eyes,
8 9, the oranges move through the window into the room.
Struggling to hold onto things they become too real.
The night takes the place of air;
you feel its weight in your dreams as repetition: the hand
that pushed you into the same wavering light
where you are always late & naked.
You know when someone else's voice spills
into yours as if you had none. And you need it
in the same way the child can't let go of the voice
which reads her to sleep among prairies & homely animals.
The footsteps recede, but she continues, makes little cow sounds
in her sleep.

In the morning you stand before a mirror
like the disfigured prizefighter
who depends now more on his dancing than his gloves.
Your place at the table should reassure you,
but your hands move like birds, fly into things,
it is all you can do to keep them still.
When you pull away from the table the bowl of fruit
is orange & white in waves. As if a ghost were in the room.
You step back from yourself with the instinct of an animal
shifting its weight.

Corner

I see trees
coming together in fence and house,
wooden hands praying rain.

Orange dust stretching
over Moorepark, covering
the sky like nylons.
Birthmarks and stars.

Beautiful corner. I put my head in,
in the truth of a right place.
Things meet here. Kiss. Cries.

I lift my head and see a rose bush
but no flower.
A bush is enough. I think
the spines of leaf
into mine
my throat
and wrists. The hallways of my body
are filled with leaves.
And I see how deer are—
forests walking into their bodies
like sounds reaching ears
in a deaf blue wind.

The afterimage of a red tiger
is blue.
Opposites meet.
Perpendiculars/prayers.
Clowns stumbling perfectly
in circus rings.

Ars Poetica

I have been reading about the great haiku artists of the 17th century
traveling together hundreds of miles
to witness a moon falling fragile yet marauding on a lake
ringed with winter, and then their bodies, huddled closely
in the wild hut, their names
nothing, because of the moonlight and animals, calling, rushing
through the woods and Matsuo Basho, through the Japanese word
for snow, falling through any letters—
all but the senses counted out.

Temple

The dogs were barking a pattern in the moonlight: figures & animals
imprinted as the stars. We talked about
building muscles and Howard Hughes; it was not money
but his not wanting to die, no more than anyone.
Packs of dogs, Jane said, have been known to run deer into the sea,
the deer swimming out through the surf
until there is no land in sight. But if animals go on,
if their mating & hunting was only part, then maybe they step out
into thick forests, and the billionaire wakes
behind blooming bougainvillea, comfortable,
but this time living simply. Still everyday I go to the gym and follow
my body in the mirrors, stretching as far towards escape
as my muscles allow.

Possibilities

Things can keep you close to them, draw you into their orbits:
the undisturbed street of a neighborhood
where a child spurs the sides of an old wall
turned into a horse.

It's what is latent in things that pulls at you like the lit up hands
of a clock, the minutes as you watch becoming larger
until each one is deafening, and the room starts to pulse.
Each object springs at you
as if you were still the little girl confined to her bedroom
swallowing her dolls' eyes like tablets.
And the cottonmouth in the creek, all invisible
snakes & aliens enter your small house.

If you knew yourself what would happen?
Would the little girl come back, the one you knew
as a child?
You might get up, bump against the sharp edge
of the nightstand, and find yourself
smiling at the quick burst of pain.
And when your eyes float out past themselves
you would be stunned by the diamonds you find within the walls.
More and more blue, more brilliant
than any snakeskin, any spaceship.

You wear the Ch'ing ivory necklace
so as always to have something when you look down.
It's the middle of the night
and everything looks distorted. You want to change
even what you want. For you're beginning to believe the possibilities.
More than you ever imagined,
running your hand down the back of your head,
everything ringing.

Banner of Fish

The sashimi comes glistening like the haiku
about the fish that swallowed another.
The fisherman who found the second body shining out
from bone & intestine, stumbled home. Green herons
plunging headlong into the water, stars
tapping trees like woodpeckers.
He lived quietly, with wonder, flying a banner of carp
to remind himself. Everything collides brightly.
So things rise out of themselves.
Sake cup/salmon, as the mind lifts, as they must always:
ovals & fish blowing through each other
like fire and wind. Thus the meaning of Basho's fish,
(which when split open revealed the Buddha it had eaten):
the herons go on feeding,
wholly conscious of the salient beauty
of their turning heads.

Singing It Back

Was there anything else besides the torn-up beaches,
reading and bougainvillea that passed through you
like a melody and you could not sing it back?
Under the thatched roof of the cabana, the ocean on & on,
the tradewinds cooling
as the water itself. Happiness,

is there a way to hold onto it? Were the Greeks right,
and fate one's character? Does this explain luck,
or the men in New York resting in tenements
rising only long enough to warm themselves?
Or could the streets seem lucky even here?

About suffering, was Auden right: did the ship sail on as Icarus fell,
or did it pass simply as one must, sometimes, walking beneath
an apartment house,
listening to a man & woman fall apart, picturing
the crushed cans of beer, the china,
hearing the stereo meant to disguise the shouts?

Because these days your sympathy only defeats you,
a string of days when you can't look
at anyone directly. The stranger next to you in line
eats at your heart, and no walk takes you away from things.
Even the love story fails: the mask of the actress tears
in her hands. Too beautiful, she is caught in the net
like one of those tropical fish, unable to complain.

But if leaving the theatre you hold onto your exhilaration—
the real sky & local bars, with the street peaceful & the heaviness
of trees still as buildings—you start singing back.

II

Revolution

The movie was about suffering; the hero a dwarf
living through a revolution.
How carefully the man behind us
must have reached for Eliot's wallet. I went out of the theatre
and the night had grown tighter, like a ring. I kept feeling,
and fingered the change in my pocket, ran my tongue
over my teeth as we walked past the window all the color blue.
"The blood of the children flowed like . . .
Like the blood of children," Neruda wrote.
In the movie the child died from the river he bathed in & drank.
If I had lived there, in Djakarta,
what could I have done?
When we turn on the floodlight at home everything's deranged:
bean poles in the swale, garden hose,
camellia & lemons; I think of the town & our thief,
and relish it all.

Next Door

Behind levelors and lace curtains, a telephone
rings, and a woman clears her throat
before answering in Spanish.
Lovely each sound cupping spring
air, knitting its weave across and down
through the flowering bottlebrush that nearly blocks
the view, from my house, of the Parkside Apartments.
There's a whole community next door.
I watch the men, mesh ball caps, checkered cook's pants,
climb into their windowless
vans in the morning and return at 5.
It's still early enough
the lumber trucks use Bay View as a shortcut.
And the children, playing, run through
the ivy-covered alley between my cindery backyard
and their apartment building,
as determined about that moment
as they may be about anything in their lives.

The West Wall

I had just left my marriage and meant to give it all up:
dining room table, tansu, stereo.
After dinner at a friend's I look through
her high-powered telescope. Alight, with a sense of order,
San Quentin sits like a space station
across Richardson Bay. And I focus, not on the marsh
with its shift of night fishers or on the knife
at Orion's hip,
but scan the west wall. A night heron flies
across a row of the barred windows.
I can see into the yellow-lit cells. Posters,
tape players, bookshelves—how meticulous men become
in confinement. The solace of what is owned.
Possessions seem always to call us. And so possessed
we anticipate or recollect world: rounder, glistening
with the lacquer of star dust.

The World Is Not Moved

The voices of boys drinking beer on Clark Street
are hard and kinetic.
The sun sets and in this florid light, the pink wall,
my fingernails, my own consciousness frightens me.
I have made myself delicate tonight.
I slice the vegetable between my thumb and finger,
its white discs fall onto one another.
The house cooling down, as shapes are muffled by nightfall
and the insects begin—their voices
almost irreverent. But they are close
to the noise & stars beating and encouraging one another.

Designs

We were talking irrigation & espaliering fig trees.
Then as we fell asleep a flash reminded us both there are good
designs, and those against it all. Against figs, spigots, eggplants
& red peppers glossy as sea stones.
Along the western edge of the garden three rocks, noses up
like triplet iguana or rockets, point toward the star, up
every morning. The dog retrieves a fallen
pear punctured with the most delicate of teeth & worm marks.
Bees. The smell of the last fruit orbits the trees; animal, vegetable,
mineral all humming like a hive
burst upon an orchard, each bee-atom
the myriad dusts gleaming over space
arranged exactly on a yellow squash blossom, the shell-
shaped corolla, though I feel large & clumsily made.

Turning From The News

Impossible to imagine so many knowing so
much does not change. A sister of St. Francis home
from Honduras or Nicaragua retells the story . . .
maybe of a vendor selling lemons, tomatillos gunned down
and left in the rubble of fruit & vegetables. Or
of the crayoned pictures posted in the schoolhouse
with the soldiers illustrated as they are. The other figures
on the flowerless ground on their knees, yellow sun
double-sized in the corner. We have heard it before, half-awake
like children listening at bedtime to the fates of rabbits &
water rats. Sometimes we feign helpfulness, but the gifts,
like Nessus' red shirt, are full of blood.
And we go on, as though true gifts, as when green turns
yellow and lemons wax and drop, will go on forever.
Forgetful. Trying to forget—the way a family bound
by death tries to loosen the knot that binds it.

Living On The Hallelujah Side

An olive angel relaxes in the sunroom with the paper,
see-through forearm on the wicker armrest.
Another calls "Elena"
from the kitchen where she's canning tomatoes,
her gauzy apron spattered with juice. A small angel
picks out pink stones on the driveway:
the radio whistles the television,
the table is set: field lilies, silverware,
napkins all trembling like water rushing through popped-
up rocks in a river. Canoes, picnickers with woven baskets
and butterfly nets. The evergreens sway outside
outside, and walls fall away to daylight.
The headlines read in reverse—white letters on black
palimpsest—PEACE & FREEDOM
in small countries, in liver-shaped and hot countries.
Millions standing up;
the river and wading to shore, the hallelujah side,
calling out like children at roll call—"Yes" or "Here".

The Hundredth One

Beauty may strip us down—
a young woman, a nude, iris & lilies arranged by the bed,
afternoon sun touching half of it.
Willingly we'll forgive the painter for leaving his wife & child.

Holding art so high it's as if our daily gestures made no
difference, but the patience of the pretty model is no less lasting
than the painting.

At times we expect too much of art, thinking
the translation of blue, and the purple shadow's blue,
will transcend this world's original light.

As on Koshiba Island where the monkeys began to wash
the sand from yellow potatoes, teaching one another, until the morning
the hundredth one knew to rinse her potatoes in the tide.

At once the whole island understood, and tribes on the mainland
learned too, within days.

Evolution could come for us like that.
Someone might place a hand on a stranger's elbow, and more kindnesses
follow like a current.

Impressionism

The painters, delighted with breasts & mango trees,
visions of paradise in the 20th century shine
and lie terribly. Matisse in a doorway
looking out, and it is lovely, the light,
and he wants to paint himself, a luminous stranger,
he wants it all through him: cinnamon peeler,
plumeria, blue of the rice field . . . but must lie.
Out of necessity. Because paradise had been broken into
with words, with gunfire,
like a woman making love to the man
who beat her once, the man not allowing her to speak
as they have sex, not to ruin
the fantasy in his mind.
Thus each beauty, a pretty child or yellow plum
leads us to all other particular beauties, like a mist—
divining water, but in a marred way.
Look how the artist hiking in the forest comes upon a girl
with half her face, though this one half shines
heavenly.

Weapons

> I know all the places where the dove lodges
> And the most natural is the head of man.
> Paul Eluard

On the freeway I pass a truck carrying pigs, the hand of the driver
waving me on almost as if the air were water,
and I cannot keep from being happy.
Outside Safeway I see this old man and he is awkward
around the kids on their bicycles. I smile at him.
He reminds me of a man in San Bernadino who must have been eighty.
We had slept in the hills. Unwashed and carrying packs,
we bought yogurt & apples in a Safeway. When we came out
he came up to us talking in Spanish,
pushing a dollar into Jim's shirtpocket.
I wanted to penetrate the world with my love of it.

I try to imagine the last design
we have on earth: irradiant light & ash—
a cow, its body leaving its ribs in a field parched by sound, the farmer
staring. The blood gone from his face, his hands filling with it.
I make promises. Pray the dove can cool the limits of air
with its wings.

Building

His white shirt falls from the bed to the floor, my sleep is lighter
than the shirt and filled with holes.
A horse kicks from within the white walls of the room.

The fog is streaming in through the sunlight, the window is open
and the small red pattern on the curtains blurs. My husband
lies exhausted from building trellises for roses and cucumbers, pleased
with his labor even as he sleeps.

5 o'clock and there is nothing more dreamlike than this
slowing down. A man working in his garden
pulls off his gloves, enjoying the sweat of his hands.
A waitress at the cafe, whose eyes are made up beautifully,
throws away the paper her customers have read all day.

I envy my husband who gets up from bed and makes himself lemonade
with lemons from our tree. If the horse kicks through the plaster, if
the room becomes filled with holes, if the world does end tomorrow, he
has prepared well.

III

Remembering About Love

Two old men come down the boardwalk in pajamas,
comfortable among tourists & galaxies,
pleased with their soft defiance.
And the child at the party who leads you on deck
to the puppy with a plum in its mouth,
is loving you.
What you've never seen before you recognize:
the night with white buildings
where the boat, harbored, whistles down stars
so that everything falling through the updraft settles
like a recurring dream. So love repeats itself.
And the child & the old pajama men
see what you see now—the city full of faces
wearing, as if second-hand suits,
the familiar smiles of others, mouths blowing
through his mouth like a smoke ring,
scent of the wisteria tinting the stranger's skin.

Light And Choice

Has my neighbor Remo, who speaks to no one but his brother,
chosen not to talk?

His vegetables radiate their own shapes & colors
while Remo casts a shadow over his green chiles.

Did his brother, Charlie, in the soft boat choose his red hair?
That boat having traveled through water,
conch shells, to where the flesh & starlight cross.
He must have. How perfectly his face belongs to him.

One brother sits watching butterflies and smoking,
while the other worries, it seems, even what the dead think.

Because Remo does not talk
the quiet around him hums: the mimosa blooming.

I wonder what can my silent neighbor do for a living?
What if this sunlight let him break into another body

appearing just as it is, another mind?, and the sulphur moths sail.

Fruit

She has reached an age where she leans far into her good luck,
into the air along the riverfront.
Slowly healing in her rooms in Buffalo, Helen has glimpsed
the angels unloading cargo on the dock,
and now still hears their chants.
In the cool terraced evening the beekeeper gleans
his prize. Workers & soldiers stream like sunlight from the hive.
His gloves glisten while the drones, dozing
deep in the braids of honey, and the carp in the pond
turn circles.
Is this the contentment the lover feels,
lying on the sheets after love, amazed by how a face
changes, yet remains the same?—hunger ripens into fruit.
Helen walks the riverbank, and the beekeeper
handles the hive like a father lifting his child.

15½

Sometimes change stays close to the body, it's the new
dreams the boy tends with his hands, the imaginary girl.
Your teenage son getting in trouble downtown
and you assure yourself he's growing-up towards whole
boy, not just golden. But you want him good again.
Your boy like young Eros with bow & arrow;
the archer trying out tequila up at the lake overlooks
old valleys—of all A's, the aquarium guppies,
of clean room, model planes, little sister. His quiver
black leather and studded, says it clearly, perfectly—
for now.

Twin Bells, Three Red Peaches

On the porch. The windless light drawing in,
John Ashdown walks past,
hat drawn over his scalp, bare
from January's chemotherapy.
His wife Lena calls to him
silently three doors down. You can hear
the twin bells attached
to the cat's collar as she circles
the house. I am
embarrassed with all I have
to say.
The Man Ray in the dining room frames
three red peaches against a green
plateau, sky blue sky. When I close
the door it is the first thing
I see. I want to race up Clorinda
like a kite carrying the heaven
depicted in the lithograph.
To John.

The Same Orbit

for W.P.

Your hello sets up an echo
and all those parallel words ending in o:
solo, duo, Pluto, halo. The sun
widening the day for a while. Tangerines & tomatoes
eclipse one another in the fruit bowl,
and I can't stop my thoughts traveling out
in little shuttles to a friend who shares
the same labor. We do the labor. Your letter arrives,
and the poems you launch in moonlight, in fog,
the unbound lyrics that defy you and fly out too far.
March, and though leaves & blossoms return green & pink,
Spring stays remote, like a planet
close only by comparison.

Pattern Language

When Nathan works with the men he stutters,
but now hauling loads of wood & rock down the mossy terraces
he sings and talks aloud on a wafer of light.
After Daphne sprang from Apollo's grasp
he loved her tree shape differently, deeply
as the moon, falling slow and clean.
So often we love past ourselves,
we imagine the cosmos as constellations of archers & dogs;
but deeper the stars circle themselves in the sky
and these curved stone stairways built by Chinese laborers in 1908.
And Nathan stacking pyramids of firewood,
rolling the wheelbarrow on a pontoon of light
up and down the hill, making this pattern his language.

California Lottery

Luck and kindness are not sisters, do not spin
or weave together in the wings of the drugstore. The girl

featherduster bristling like the mignon tail of a gamebird
from her back pocket, has no
blessing from beyond. Possesses radiance only

as she taps the purchase on the register, calls out the figures
in cents, and then, beginning with the heaviest,
packs each item as if these sundries—epsom salts,
fluorescent bulb—were samples from the moon.

And when I ask for a ticket, pay my dollar
towards whatever bounty a million more might bring,
she so earnestly separates the lone slip from the rest—
as a sportsman would pull from the carcass the offal
the hunter might neglect—I stand already winning.

But the circles do not ring. No three queens, no lassoed aces.

I leave without passage to luxury—no date palms, bunched,
spring-fed, above my secluded bungalow.

Hammer Then An Angel

The rain refreshes the dot-like birds, euphoric in the grass:
the grass no more than passive.
No blade disturbed by any other, like a man and a woman
who pass each other daily, brushing shoulders
but never ruining their silence. The grass absorbs
the sound of the birds' wings fluttering.
Jean's husband Sali died Tuesday,
the children doing everything for her
in the way old women despise.
If she does anything it is alone.
What in her is nourished by their kindness?
Towards the East Bay the clouds continue to form
and fall apart. The ones you see as ships, the horse's head,
the one you see first as a hammer then an angel.
I think of Dickinson watching clouds, her narrow hands spreading wide
& wide against her window.
Do we make the unbearable a gate, or how else
get through loneliness?

We Have This Harmony,

the angry parts are songs;
the geese & children and men & women
sing with their mouths open twice, as they appear to friends.
The neighborhood is startlingly luminous. Yellow worlds
leak out through windows, a woman leans against a fence
on a lit-up corner. I turn the radio loud.
As if one part of me, like a husband or wife,
could keep from listening to the other. This woman and the dark
blue field where two geese move towards her. The white one
hissing at her, wings open like a five-point star. The one bullet
she fires.
There's a man in your poem
bent over a kitchen table, drumming his fingers.
The walls are still.
A child's hand strokes his head, but any minute
the man might wreck everything.
Coda. The song keeps crossing over. We have this harmony.

Heavy Equipment

Under the bur-bearing sycamores, where the blind woman
on her husband's arm has begun her mid-morning
walk, my other neighbor's new wife pushes
her baby's stroller. He's at work at the brickyard.
A contractor for twenty years
who, after a long illness, let his business go.
The wooded hills he saw from his sickbed,
the sun up and down, did not promise him enough.
Where each cell was a window
instead the body became a lightless room.
I think of Van Gogh writing to his brother, Theo,
how he must paint the landscapes constantly
because tomorrow the pain may worsen.
Now Jim would rather run heavy equipment,
move slate and cinder block around the sun-shot
yard, than build new houses. This man
who I knew as his own boss—working late,
joking with his crew.

Walks Of Life

1. Weight Lifter

His lips and nose were disfigured so he looked like a deer;
when he raised and lowered the heavy stacks he wanted
the strangeness healed. The whole gym was about redemption,
the body fruit ripening—
a peach set to blush on the spirit's sill.
The fibers of his muscles, orange & sand-colored, as in textbooks
stretched over one another. Various & shapely.
His mind guided the weight settled in his grasp,
like a thought carried since childhood, the god Atlas
supporting the globe.
And this was how he held to goodness, a weight
curled to the brain, with Mercury running the footpaths
of his body, begging the cells to expand.
Crossing the bar over his chest, the pectorals hardened,
but beneath, the heart creased then opened on itself.
Daily he practiced with as many strangers and friends
as he remembered to, saying silently, I love you, feeling the ridged
shells of the turtles underneath him.

2. *Psychic Healer*

Men at the lunch counter, the whole diner
appeared to him within another diner
where things sifted like the grains of rice in the salt.
As he ate he wondered how the apple was altered
by his organs—lay in an orchard, stunned
with the acceleration of ripening energy, with red fruit & seed
almost pure black, until he felt his thoughts
in his tongue, his digestion.
Around strangers he saw the colored lights,
and watched the dead climb in waves.
He let his eyes drift like the passers-by,
and went into trance as other men
might read the paper or drink a beer.
Through his third eye he saw the wavering, a spirit
floating like the hat of a drowned man, and was taken again
by the power of metaphysics:
that everything hidden could be revealed.

3. Masseuse

She liked best when they fell asleep, rocking
the torso, slightly, mutely, then cradling the head,
she pictured a diver coming up
through cliffs of coral, debris, sunfish; swimming,
losing the body where the water began.
Anatomy she felt superficial, latissimus & liver
no more like their illustrations than real countries
the colors on a map. Muscles bunched and organs drifted
like boats anchored loosely.
At her table she had a wrestler's wide stance,
but her touch she wanted deep, tender, a tender
to carry off the heaviest cargo, her hands discovering
the body's freight: stories eased from around the heart,
an accident, the too-much-drinking—
in clenched trapezius, deltoids; learning the length
of the quadriceps as if she were a mermaid,
curious, in love with a shipwrecked sailor, as if
she knew no geography nor spoke a word.

4. Beautician

She tells herself beauty lives within, as in the fables—forest
boy or river girl springing
from behind a homely beast's veneer—yet she lingers
over the pretty redhead's reflection,
the fiery charm,
shimmery as the tropical hues she uses to make up the eyes,
the lips, seamed halves of peach, mango.
Straightening her colors, scissors, brushes, sprays, clips,
her poise, her stories & gossip, she's ready for the ones
wanting a change, and isn't that everyone
who'll slip on her shiny shaken-out gown? Lightening,
painting, trimming, as if the lovelier they are,
she is—trying to please, yet not be taken
wholly by appearance.
But when a girl leaves truly dazzling her breath takes
off like one bird after the gorgeous feathers of another,
after the pink-crested parrot, half bird, half nymph.

5. Garbage Collector

Often he comes to the place the garden hose is coiled,
the dog's bowl kept—the dog he cajoles
with biscuits and whatever name he's overheard
its master save him with.
Grown comfortable, as he has with melon rinds & tuna fish cans,
assuming everyone thinks him half there, limited—
like a creature on the sea floor, dim & bivalved,
that can't touch more showy phylum.
Not riding the waves for Venus,
he is Neptune of backwater, brackish waste.
Nostalgic for bygone summers: shadeless lamps & unsprung sofas
left out on the streets, when his route
led house to house, not to complexes with swimming pools
and idle girls uncovering bikinis by 9 A.M., giggling
shrugging off his manhood. Never at ease with this
as he does his job, shrimp, sea shells, sea foam
sliding from his shoulders.

6. Zoo Keeper

Every decision he saw as right: the bear no longer in her cage
could find herself dancing,
chained to a man from the circus,
while the wildebeests in thousands flashed across
the floor of the sky, rippling in stripes,
innocent of the lioness watching. But, he supposed,
not even the slower one, singled out for the kill, witnessing
its flesh pulled from its hips, questioned the herd's choice
of savanna.
In the aquarium he fed the lampreys, streaming
like lead grey ribbons, and saw all the possibilities
displayed like the spectrum: the many lovers and cities.
But what if he had pursued the remarkable blonde in the bookstore,
had moved to the city with orange light salvaging the ghetto
at sunset, the city with the job
selling or buying, he was sure, one could never know.
He dreamt about the bear, no longer pacing her square
at the zoo. She appeared lumbering through a melody.

7. Geologist

Working for the mine owner he delighted in every new vein,
the wild line of metal running like a wire
through his body.
And like a newlywed entering his first house—
who sees the mantle, banister, hardware,
promise good long life—
still those melons seeded with quartz dazzled him.
The green aloe rays seemed to grow
out of the ticking the lizard made, surprising him
into memory: the boy quartering lizards like apples,
the stones his own size loosened by lever & fulcrum over the cliff.
Alone on the plain below the mesa he accepted loneliness
and the pressure cradling fossils & ferns.
He hoped working with rocks, metals,
gems, granite might extend his time into theirs.

8. Patient

After a sneeze the dizziness keeps her spinning
like a globe in a schoolroom. The green pill winks,
the orange one goes down a burning ship.
She has chosen Christopher, patron of travelers, as if the saint
might guide her out of her body, free
to wander. In daydreams she's her own twin sister, tanned
& freckle-faced, suitcase stamped with pyramids,
kangaroos, Paris.
Housebound; her few good days: whistles coming closer—
the train she's waited for at all those clinics, holding out
her prescription. Once aboard she'll be just another tourist
fanning herself in a warm compartment. Out the window
blur of leaf monkeys & Brahman.
Though sure happiness runs counter to the body
she follows the train as it speeds to a glimmer.

9. Gospel Singer

She wants His tongue the wick in the dim lamp
of her mouth, though she lights the church with gospel
she worries where He shines as she gossips in the market.
An alto, she holds her body like a tower,
a lighthouse—receives and sings His signals.
Sometimes she sees Jesus shepherding His lambs, watchful,
almost feminine; then He's a leopard, pouncing,
heavy as iron wrapped in a flag.
Sundays it seems the Holy Spirit could be anyone
among the congregation. And she struggles not to judge
the grocer in the second pew and his two cronies,
or the palm reader with her eyebrows sketched in.
"I was a stranger and you welcomed me,"
she whispers. She sings so that the one she loves least
she loves as much as she does God.

IV

Abbott's Lagoon

for M.L.

The refrigerator in that cottage rumbled
and we had our pattern: to make love, open it (almost afraid
to stop eating), then love again.
In the dunes gulls and marbled godwits
dwarfed by herds of dinosaur-pelicans; the lagoon's
ebbing reach, the headland cut away to the water
like a slice of cake: pink, ginger, platinum.
Posted on long, hinged legs, shore-feeding tinbirds
worked welded beaks, as if imitating the man-made:
fishing tackle, the birdwatchers' tripods.
Then dozens rushed along the shoreline,
like surf.
And the two of us, there, a paradigm of lovers, not
a man who waited for his children outside
his old house and a woman consulting lawyers.
Azure heat rippling the sandbars—
kinetic waterfowl and meals of fish.

McClure's Beach

Above the sunset-washed cliffs covered with graffiti
the size Jupiter might have lettered
as proof to Juno, the gold sea-light made coins
of the undersides of air-borne headland birds.
Later in your room the jazz
by a musician I'd forgotten (I recognized the clarity,
the verve), unheard since on another coast, years ago,
love's small fires proved as inexhaustible.

Enough

We feel the grass on our knees
in the grass, we look at the cows. Enough
to love, to take a walk, to lie
on our backs. The few large stars.

I remember myself walking
to Hamburg over
the bridge at 18 Mile Creek,
after a swim
for pie and milk at Beehlers',
to spin on a green stool
till my body went weightless
my tennis shoes smoked till the waitress
touching me on the hand said,
"Enough dear".
And for the first time all
day long it was.
Halfway home I could still feel
that tap on my hand
ring like a splash.

And now my hands, the grass, the black & white cows—
electric. And there's nothing
I'd change now
now when I love you,
no molecule not touched.

Grace

I was mistaken about it. Thinking it meant elegance,
balance. Mistaken about you, man who breaks
and loses things when you visit. Man whom I love undressing
me when we've pulled the shade
on the party next door at the Parkside Apartments,
and the bedroom expands, a universe, furniture
shifting towards the red of twilight.

You'll knock at the door
and soon some object, some delicate material wafer,
will be torn or misplaced: a rice paper blind,
a contact lens.
But whatever of me lies against you disproves boundaries
and surfaces, as there are only depths,
and the lost possessions rest among fragments on the ocean floor.

Orange Blossoms

Just before sleep we argue, vying like two sloops
for the same lane out. We feel judged
because we judge.
Soon words are held back, tightly,
like beach umbrellas tied up in a storm.
And when we finally come to sleep, this world imitating
the other, a migrant warbler
models seven notes on the fragrance of citrus—
the unsteady whistle of a boat
moored to its drifting.

The Force Of His Sadness

His face in the lamplight, like a coin
embossed with the gold cheekbones
of an emperor. My husband
nurses himself, in bed with tea,
reading garden books. He looks small
pulling his robe tighter, tilting his head.
I am up on the hill and he cannot see me
chronicling his sorrow.
I can feel my cells unthread,
the red iron in my chest ground down and pulled
like metal filings to his sadness.

Squaw Valley Without You

As if you were on this walk, even when I sing
you stay with me; horses bunched and grazing
on the floor of the sky, top-shaped pine cones
come to rest in the drifts of field flowers
in these ice-cut sierras.
There was that valley through Privas.
Under a half-there Roman bridge, remember?,
eating cherries and drinking milk
that tasted of hazelnuts. And suddenly, covered
by a net of blue provincial butterflies,
we had to shake ourselves loose.

A stand of colossal flagpoles, their weighted lines
tolling, are bell towers. Towers ringing
in this meteor-showering August signal towards
all those stars not falling.
All those possible listeners. Sending out our best:
Mozart, and Schubert's skyrocketing trout,
Vermeer's transparent figures, O'Keefe's
amaryllis—half petal, half bone; blue pine, blue
net; those stopped moments on the road.

Hunger

All the way to the mountains I used the radio and
ate sugar to stay awake, touching myself where want
intersected with beauty speeding by.
Now, as I undress, the view makes me hungry again,
our sex lingering, forgive me, like the sense one has,
almost anywhere in the world this magnificent, of the first ocean
tingling with limulus, bivalve, blue anemone—limitless
incline of pines, the light, titanic,
translate back to your description of this valley.
I look from the wide rim of the cirque to my flat stomach.
Food works no better than sleep. Hunger. I remember a thin man
begging in a great city, wearing himself out, my hand
diving for change, insistent as an insect at a light.

We Women

And now the red tools of the heart work,
as I did, all day in the garden, turning the heavy soil
with my soft muscles.
I am in a house among houses with steps, kitchen light,
other women standing on the porch in their pajamas.
I hold a book against my chest
like the closely held fan of an oriental woman.

My sister-in-law puts on her ragged silk kimono, her babies
asleep by now, her husband working late.
She has been sanding the ceiling of her kitchen, preparing to paint. Tired,
she checks on her children, whom, with the light
touch of the back of her hand, she touches.
No amount of sanding or blue paint will ease Carol's worries:
we must work with different tools.

Inevitable Her Hunger

My niece understands Oliver is more loveable.
Because of his smallness, and he so much shier
than she ever was. But the housekeeper must nod
to assure her she's not invisible at the kitchen table.
She loves her brother.
They tease and hold one another watching tv
in the room with the dinoasaur curtains. The dog
ate most of the Italian plastic watch
I gave her, but Tuesday's Oliver's birthday
and how can I give her the present? He'll enjoy
the brontosaurus cookie cutters. She'll find some recipe.
As it's inevitable, her hunger.

The Child

Working outdoors, carrying the tubes of wire from the garden
and Oliver comes.
At two, always wanting an orange when he visits and going right away
to his uncle's desk for the colored stickers he knows about.
These are his now.
I have the man named Homer, and his wife
who helped me make cakes out of soap suds. And the Cuban who lived in
        Buffalo
and always gave me the band from his cigar.
The expressions are gone,
the faces I don't remember, but it is something that I touch
when I don't even mean to.
All the distinctions are less than that.
Oliver too, making up his,
pleasing me without saying a word, coming up to me—
starting to hug me without stopping.

Pure And Indiscriminate

The spinach leaves flower, the peas, planted foolishly
on the west side of the trellis, toughen.
And above these twin windows the walls are strewn
with old webs, insect parts—motionless
as the piled-high chassis in a junkyard.
Overlooking the lot the operator salvages
what seems best. A man with a European accent who loses
his temper, but then a second lever adjusts
and there he is, the same man, my father.
The signs all here, like flowers going to seed, like
the compost hot with life, the wind
reshaping the trees the way a magnet sweeps up
a clump of metal shavings. Pure and indiscriminate
as memory, which bears both bright gardens and the day
growing darker and darker. Darkness
and heartache indelible: a birthmark.

The Light All Inside Them

Quietly, like a sailor whistling alone on deck,
I walk to the back of the house, turn on a light
then shut the window. The last handful of wind
on my face wakes me up, I write to my father
in Buffalo, who sleeps the same light
way I do. I see the snowdrifts cresting in waves
against his dark red house, his same thin
bathrobe hanging on the closet door. Blood,
I say to myself. Always the arc of the diver
is luminous, and so it is with the wind
and light. The bottom of a ship glides
over the ceiling where I can see more
clearly, as if the room were lit by a fisherman
harvesting a hundred thousand
fish as they swim toward the light, bright and sexual.

Two, Three

The light hammers tap against the fleshy bells. A boy—
eleven, twelve—rides a train from Vienna with a fuchsia
on his lap.
It's wonderful, my father says, how memory
feels as if you're alive two or three times.
I think about the brain like a flower, like a tent
with two rooms, and whorls of stars just above the center pole
make shadows on the canvas. I count the loops, the rope
tied to the green earth.
Deer stop mid-stream, each looking in another direction—
the way the boy bored with geometry
traces triangles on the ceiling, or draws rabbits
with ears pressed flat against cone-shaped heads
in the margin of a notebook.
What if we did live twice—like a thought
pulling away from another orbit?
It was his birthday, my father on his way to the country:
the low ghetto houses, a farmer with a rabbit cage,
forest whirring by the moving compartment.
His thoughts make him hold his mouth—his whole world
rising like a planet.

Bells

for P.M.

New hexagrams drift steadily down. In the storm, hushed,
snowed-in from the grocery, the shoe repair on Buffalo,
you go about the day, listening
for the plow to come and make a hallway of the road.

Behind the picture window in a flurry of slowness—
you spell out your every gesture, like a magician
revealing the trick, say of opening the newspaper.

Before the refrigerator you pause, then lift out two cold ovals,
and finally (as physics there seems an altered state),
when the water boils, coddle the eggs three soft minutes.

Retired; breakfast lasts all afternoon. An old upright
blanketed with bills, in the closet an accordian
freighted from Europe forty years ago;
you play the radio and with the terrier
racing through the house—shuttered square at the edge
of a small town in a big state. Zero & below the only prediction.

Joy has come to you, unhurriedly,
and like the mirage gleaming in the desert that proves
a true oasis. Housebound, snowbound, nightfall hidden
but for bells downtown, their crescent-shaped,
moon-shaped sounds.

Sail

Every day I keep feeling I must give.
I want to walk this way: mostly all light with my face undisguised.

And there stands Franz again & the house in Holland & the tree—
disappearing in its rush of gold confetti.
I have thought about his room, his clothes . . .
all the things that stay here.

What is there in the way death comes and leaves us behind
that stops me years later, like a child about to join in the games,
but called too small?

Can Franz see me and my face?
In the river light as they bathe & brush their hair
where the stars swim out, we mean less.
As the dead wash, the world dissolves on their skin.

I see this sail coming closer all the time, along the shore, pines.
Fish painted rose-colored on the sides of the boat.
Sunsets like red hats, angels . . .
I hear the crew singing,
and want to be the one note carried, higher.

Heaven is moving towards me and every day I'm afraid,
and ask myself who might need my love.
All this struggling to be good.

Uncle Franz wades to his hips in the quieting water,
not worrying about his children, without the suit he had made in Berlin.

Precious Few

In April some fish would fly.
My mother could sit hours above
Twin Falls
and watch a thousand shiners jump.

The few that made it past
1945 had to
swim like seals
heads glossy, bodies forgotten.
Just a cold smoke around them.
No wine, no sunny cows.

Uncle Franz told me
how he was held by Germans,
how he talked to his hands about his babies.
Feeling their faces
on the dirt walls they
would keep jumping
into his arms
until my grandmother bribed a guard.
Even taking the tortoise shell
from her hair. I

barely remember her
except one night driving
the Skyway
over the furnaces of Bethlehem Steel
her face closed like a nasturtium.
My mother rolled the windows
but you could still smell steel,
and she asked what
all those rubies were
and was the city burning.

Trespass

I listen to its oriole, its jay, then watch the mockingbird I know
by the white fingers on its wing, veer
onto the gutter and walk into the coolness under the red tile roof.

Hot and cool. Like the two sides of my mother's door:
the breezy green hallway and her room—
dark pink rosettes on the walls. The clarity of physical boundaries.

Inside the light is a nail I keep bending with my heavy hammer.
How many times have I damned and then forgiven her,
her leaving—the garage door shut, the car filling with gas?

Just now the mockingbird lands near the ranunculus.
I think of the mother I knew as a little girl. Finally
recognizing how unforgiving forgiveness is.

Presence And Absence

I know you are watching too.
Watching the wind. The leaves, a bird caught at an odd angle,
the heaviest purple figs blown down.
That when you left it was just to be invisible,
not absent. The peaches are past, the grapes, and pears.
Your pain. I keep thinking about pain,
how fine its edges can be slicing fresh & deep—
until I can think of nothing else, like a lover lying in bed alone
satisfied and hungry.
The thin coma of white vapor collecting in the sky
reminds me how self-conscious you were.
How I want to join you when I want nothing,
but keep wanting. How the late light forms,
its planes & intervals on the wall partly obscured by trees.

The Brittingham Prize in Poetry

The University of Wisconsin Press Poetry Series

Ronald Wallace, General Editor

Places/Everyone
Jim Daniels

Talking to Strangers
Patricia Dobler

Saving the Young Men of Vienna
David Kirby

Pocket Sundial
Lisa Zeidner

Slow Joy
Stefanie Marlis